YOUR wild CELEBRATION

We acknowledge the Traditional Owners of the country on which we live, learn, play and create. We are grateful to First Nations people for being custodians of the land for countless generations. A particular appreciation goes to the Peramangk people, the Traditional Owners of the land upon which this book was created.

YOUR wild CELEBRATION

nature play activities for Christmas,
Easter, birthdays + more

Brooke Davis

with photography by Megan Crabb

This book is for the
Nature Warriors.
Yes, that includes you!

A huge heartfelt thank you goes to the wonderful children in this book and their parents. Thank you Milly and Archer Davis, Paige Crabb, Delilah Stoeckel, Felix Paskett, Joseph and Amelia, Levi and Myah, and Lucas and Megan Cheung.

CONTENTS

CELEBRATING THE
wild way

There are a handful of events throughout the year that generate a great amount of excitement. Christmas, Easter and birthdays are usually amongst the most highly anticipated celebrations for children and grown ups alike!

While we love to celebrate these occasions and many more, increasingly we want to do so in a sustainable way - consuming mindfully and not generating excess waste. In this book we provide ways you can reduce your impact on the environment and have an amazing celebration!

This book is divided into five sections, but this does not mean these activities are not transferable to other occasions. For example, you can apply the same environmental concepts from the birthday party preparation section to any celebration such as a baby shower, wedding or school fête. Similarly, if you do not celebrate Christmas or Easter, you could adapt these activities to other occasions that are important for your family.

We have also included a section on celebrating the seasons. You might like to do this on the first day of each season, or on the seasonal solstice or equinox. Your local area might not experience the four distinct seasons described in this book, but you can adapt the activities to suit your location. Perhaps you can select four times of the year and spend a day or week celebrating all the wonderful fauna and flora that are native to your local area.

You will notice that we don't include many human-made items such as sticky tape in our activities. We all have a responsibility to mindfully choose what materials we create with. Our goal for the activities in our books is to have minimal impact on the environment. You will be able to compost the items you make at the end of their life, perhaps after removing a couple of elements (such as wire or synthetic yarn). By choosing materials that can be composted rather than go to landfill, we can reduce our impact on this beautiful planet we share.

For more nature play activities and books, visit yourwildbooks.com

A NOTE ON SAFETY

Some of the activities present an element of risk, which is necessary to develop our children. But please ensure they are supervised at all times. It is vital to assess the risks specific to your situation and act to keep everyone safe. Please consider each individual's unique abilities when undertaking these activities. We particularly advise caution and commonsense when using natural materials because they can be unpredictable.

* after the party,
  please plant ends
  ... in your garden
  * ... when the
  flowers grow
  Bury 1cm deep
  and water. ♥

...ner is 6! YAY!

...e join us for a

...TURE PLAY PARTY!

IT'S

PARTY TIME

party
PLANNING

WELCOME TO OUR
NATURE PLAY PARTY
-
NATURE HUNT
WANDS
YOUR WILD QUIZ
PAINT & POT PLANTS
CAKE

preparation + STYLING

preparation
+ STYLING

THINGS TO GATHER

*Table and table cloth
(we used large pieces
of second-hand fabric)*

Platters and simple food

Compost bucket

Vases and foraged flowers

*Glasses with leaf name tags
(write on leaves with a
paint pen, punch a hole in
the leaf, attach with string)*

Plates and cutlery

*Reusable decorations such
as a party garland (page 18)*

Choose **food** items that don't require a lot of last minute preparation. We served fruit, popcorn and cake. Provide a compost bucket for food scraps.

Forage **flowers** and foliage from your garden and the local area. Arrange them in different size vases.

For entertainment choose two **games** to play and two **craft** activities. See a list of suggested party games and craft ideas on page 114. Also allow time for free play.

Plan for the party to be plastic free. Decorate with reusable items. Use glasses, plates and cutlery from home, or borrow from friends. Choose second hand if you do need to purchase some items.

Above all, keep the party simple, start planning early and use the checklist on page 114.

seed PAPER

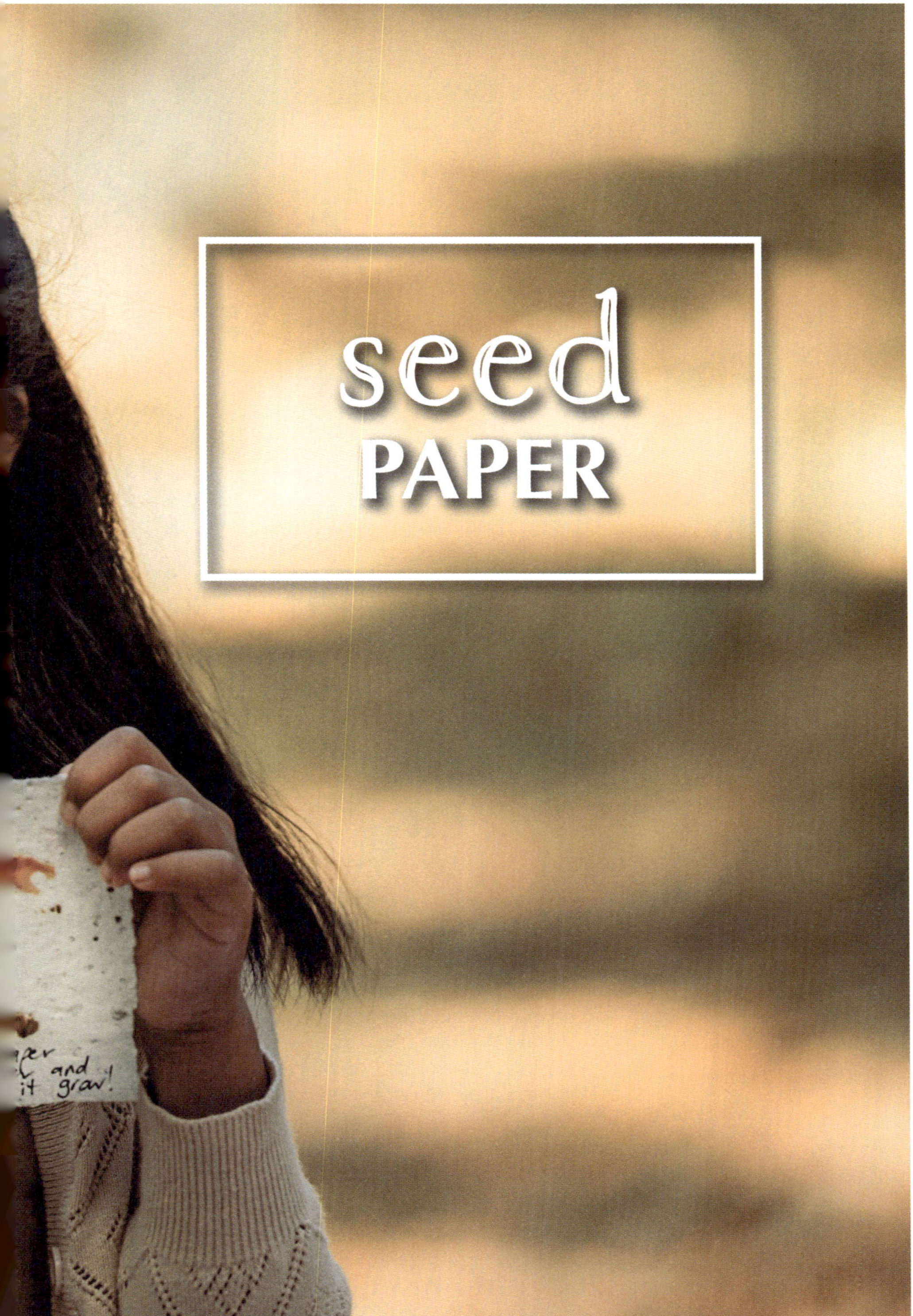

seed
PAPER

Protect your workspace with a towel. Rip the scrap paper into small pieces, put into the blender and cover generously with water. Blend until a runny pulp forms.

Add the pulp to a tub of water, approximately 10 litres, and mix well. Place the paper making frame into the tub and lay the frame flat under the water. Lift the frame up keeping it flat so that the pulp is evenly spread over the whole frame. Allow the water to drain out.

Remove the top part of the frame and sprinkle seeds and petals evenly over the pulp. Lay a piece of calico fabric over the seeds on the paper pulp, then flip it over onto the towel. Remove the mesh frame and cover the pulp with a piece of absorbent felt. Use the roller to push the felt onto the pulp and extract as much water as possible. Remove the felt and set the paper aside to dry on the calico. Once fully dry, remove the calico.

party
GARLAND

party
GARLAND

THINGS TO GATHER

Fabric

Pinking sheers

Scissors

Cotton twine or ribbon

Masking tape

Sewing machine or needle and tread (optional)

Use pinking sheers to cut the fabric into the desired shape for your flags. You can use fabric you've coloured with natural dyes (page 26), re-purposed fabric such as old pillow cases, second-hand or store bought fabric. You can also combine this activity with another from our book *Your Wild Imagination*, where you use nature to print on the fabric.

Use scissors to cut a small slit into the top two corners of each flag. Cut a length of twine about twice as long as the combined length of the flags. Wrap a piece of masking tape around the end of the twine to keep it from fraying. Thread the twine through the slits in a weaving pattern (in-out-in-out). Tie a knot after each slit to keep the flags from moving along the twine.

Alternatively, you can secure the flags onto a length of ribbon using a sewing machine or sew by hand.

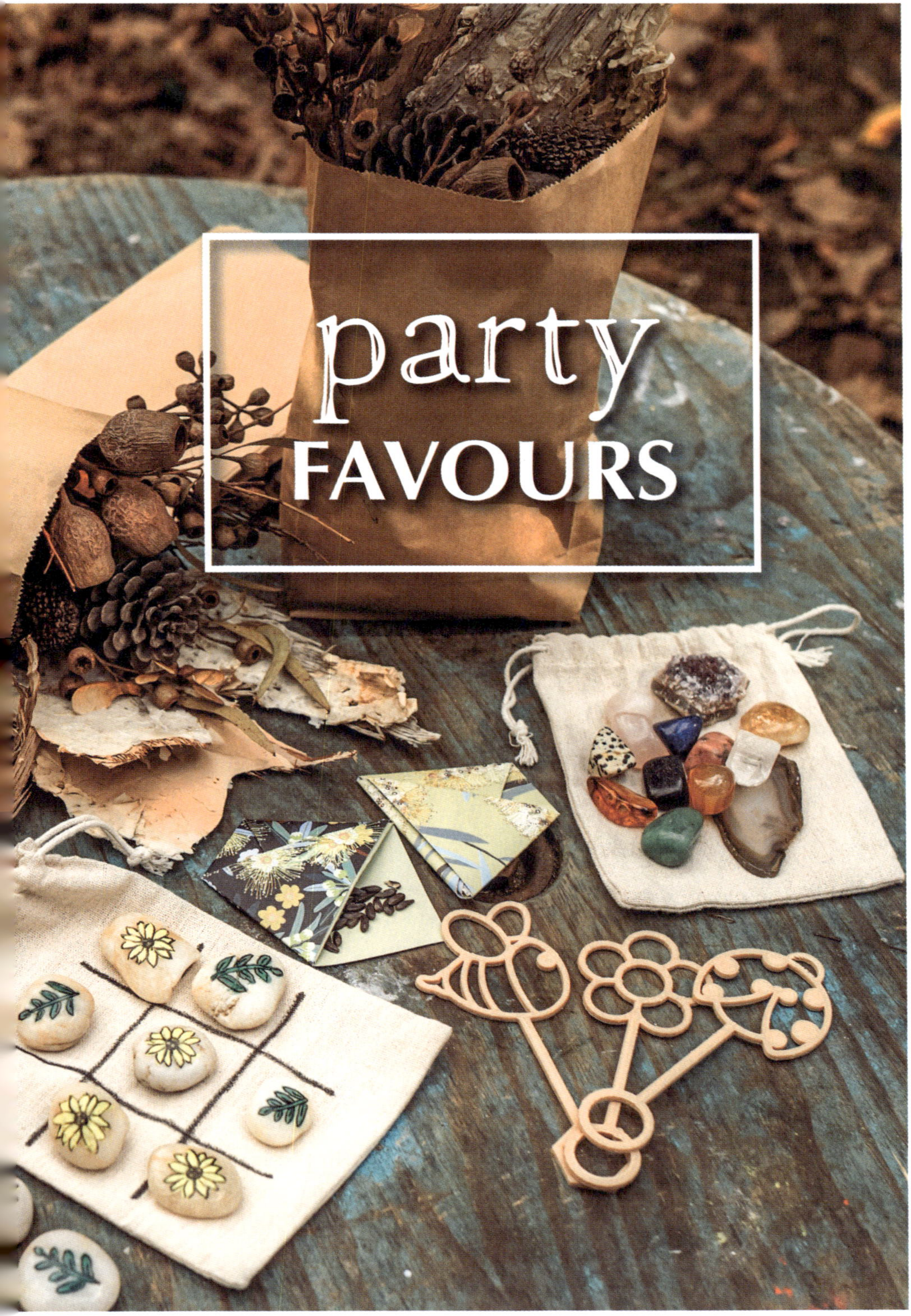
party
FAVOURS

party
FAVOURS

THINGS TO GATHER

Colourful paper cut into 15cm squares

Scissors

Seeds

Masking tape

Pen

Choose a plastic free party favour for your guests. Some ideas include a bag full of nature, eco-friendly bubble wand, a crystal, a nature tic tac toe game (see previous page) or a little origami seed envelope.

To make an origami envelope, fold a piece of paper in half into a triangle and have the longest side facing you.

Take the lower right corner and fold across to the middle of the opposite side, so there is a straight edge along the top. Repeat with lower left corner.

Tuck the first layer of the triangle at the top of card into the pocket you made in the previous step.

Fill with seeds and a small note to explain how to grow the seeds. Secure with a piece of masking tape and write the guest's name on the envelope.

fabric
DYEING

fabric
DYEING

THINGS TO GATHER

*Various natural dyes
(instructions on page 112)*

100% cotton fabric

Bowls

Gloves (optional)

*Gum nuts, rocks
or seed pods*

String

Scissors

Rubber bands

** Due to the absence of a colour
fixing agent, we don't recommend
using natural dyed fabric for clothing
as the colour could transfer.*

Use natural dyes to create your own unique, reusable fabric for present wrapping and party bunting.

Fold, twist and scrunch the fabric in the way of your choice. Add rubber bands or string to keep it secure. You might like to place gum nuts or rocks into the fabric and secure them individually with rubber bands.

Submerge the fabric in a bowl of natural dye, pushing it down with your hands so it absorbs the liquid. Use gloves if you wish.

Leave the fabric to soak for 30 minutes for a light colour, or overnight for a deeper colour. Rinse the fabric briefly under cold water, squeeze out excess moisture and hang to dry. You might like to iron the fabric once it's dry.

For other present wrapping ideas see page 13 and 48.

party
DAY

NATURE HUNT

FLYING INSECT

☑

FEATHER

☑

SNAIL OR SLUG

☑

BIRD

☐

CONE OR SEED PO...

☑

GRASS

☑

COLOURFUL LE...

☑

FLOWER

☑

CRAWLING INSECT

☑

Y SHAPED STICK

☑

SPIDER WEB

☑

BUTTERFLY

☑

nature HUNT

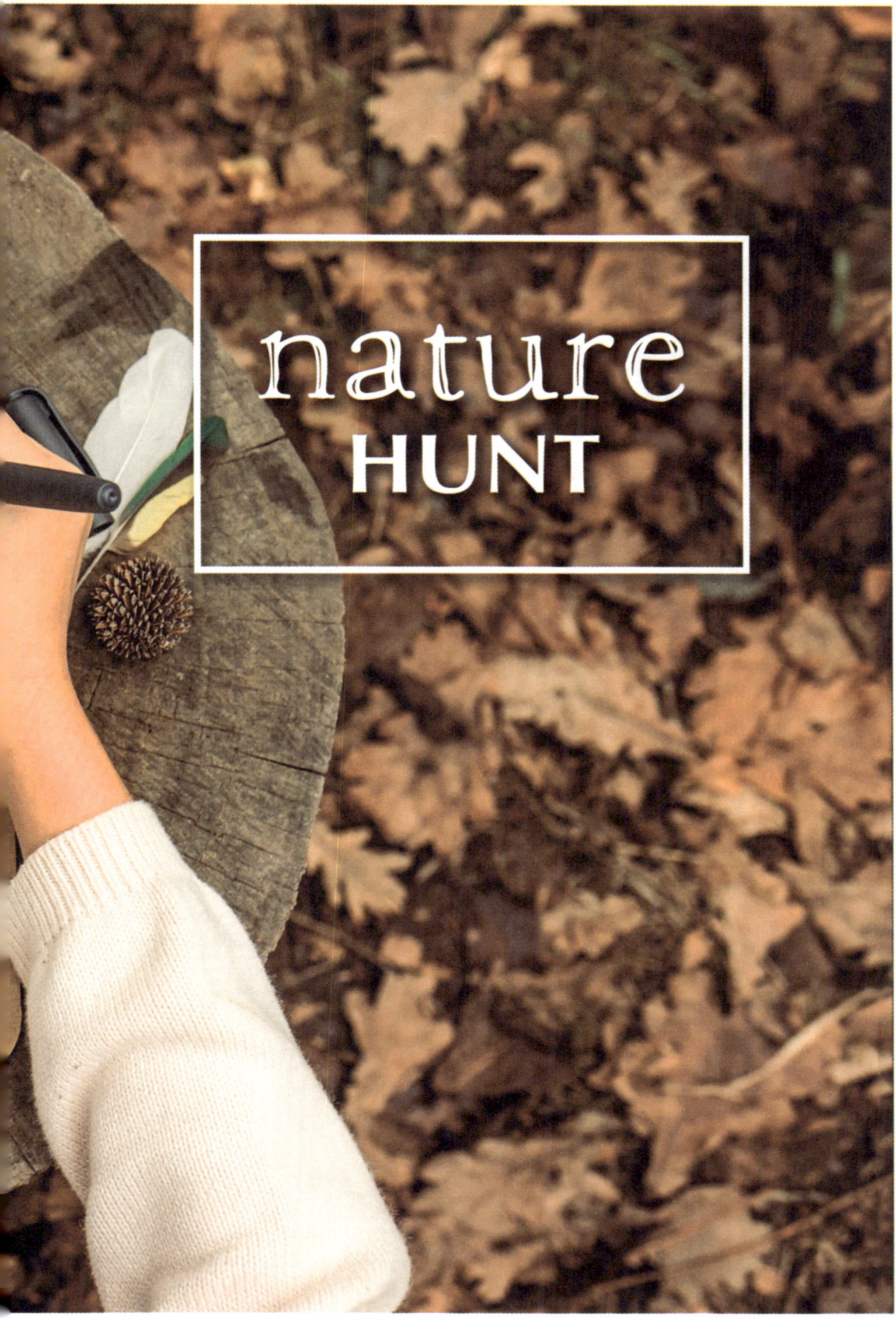

nature
HUNT

THINGS TO GATHER

*Printed nature hunt page
(see page 113)*

Pens

Clipboards (optional)

This game can be played individually or in pairs. Provide each person or pair with a nature hunt game board and a pen. Using a clipboard is helpful but not necessary; cardboard would also work well.

Define a search area within which participants try and find as many of the items as possible. Each time they find one of the items, tick it off the game board, or pick it up if it is safe to do so. Please respect Mother Nature and do not disturb living plants, animals or insects.

After approximately 5-10 minutes, gather in a group and see who has ticked the most items off their game board. Ask each person or pair to share their favourite item from the nature hunt and why they thought it was interesting.

YOUR
wild
QUIZ

YOUR • wild QUIZ

THINGS TO GATHER

*One set of
'Your Wild Quiz' cards*

*Purchase cards from
yourwildbooks.com
or make your own from
the guide on page 115*

*This game is suitable
for 2 or more players
aged 5 and up*

Nominate one person as the Quiz Master, who will be in charge of reading out the cards. They can also play the game if they wish. Shuffle each deck separately and place them face down. The Quiz Master picks up a card from the top of the **Descriptions** deck and reads it aloud. Then they pick up a card from the **Letters** deck and announces it. For example, *"A bird starting with the letter R."*

It is up to the players to think of something that fits this description and say it aloud. The first person to correctly call out their answer is handed the letter card. Continue until there are no more letter cards remaining. The person with the most letter cards at the end of the game is the winner.

Some description and letter combinations might be tricky. If after two minutes no one has announced a correct answer, then adjectives (describing words) can be used instead. For example 'Running emu' or 'Red parrot'.

38

party
WANDS

party
WANDS

THINGS TO GATHER

Fresh and dried grass

Sticks

Wool

Scissors

Wire and pliers

Flowers

Feathers

Wands make the perfect party activity because they ignite imaginations and encourage free play.

To make a **heart shape wand**, take a small bunch of fresh grass and secure it to the end of the stick with wool. Then divide the grass into two even bunches and bend them over in opposite directions to make a heart shape. Secure the grass with more wool.

To make a **star shape wand**, take one piece of long, dried grass and fold it into a five pointed star with one piece longer than the others. Secure the joins with wire and tie the longest side of the star onto a stick with wool.

Decorate the wand with flowers, feathers and wool.

pots
+ PLANTS

pots
+ PLANTS

Use the paint pens to decorate a terracotta pot.

Lay a piece of paper in the bottom of the pot to stop the soil from falling through the drainage hole.

Add a small amount of soil on top of the paper and then put the seedling or plant in the pot. Top up the sides of the pot with more soil and press it down with your hands until the plant is secure. If using seeds, add more soil and then bury the seeds as described on the packet.

Ask the guests to water the plants generously once they take them home.

These pots can also double as a party favour and it is an activity that can also be done at baby showers, bridal showers and school fêtes.

wild
CHRISTMAS

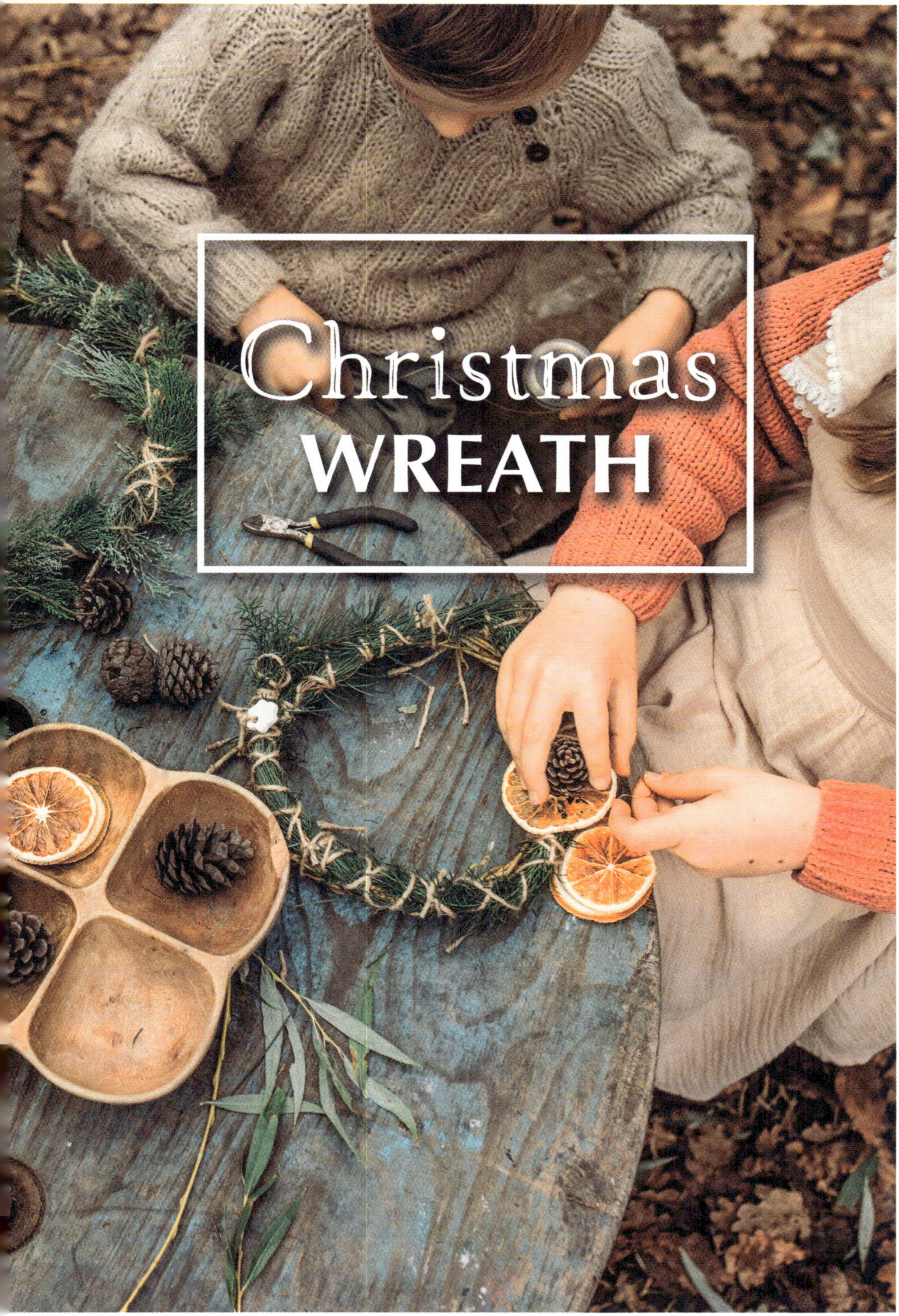

Christmas WREATH

Christmas
WREATH

Strip the leaves off the willow branches. Form a circle with the branch and weave the ends in and out of the circle. Continue adding pieces of willow and weaving it together until the wreath is the strength you desire.

Make a sausage shape with small bunches of pine and wrap string around the outside to bind it all together. Attach the pine sausage to the wreath base with string.

Alternatively, gather small bunches of pine and attach them to your wreath base using wire and pliers.

Use string or wire to attach the decorative pieces of nature where you'd like them on the wreath.

Add a small loop of string to the top of the wreath to hang it up on your front door.

stick
STAR

stick
STAR

THINGS TO GATHER

Sticks

Secateurs

Wire and pliers

Small pine cones

Holly

Pine needles

Small bells

String or wool

Scissors

Find six sticks and trim them to the same length using the secateurs. Make a triangle with three of the sticks and secure the corners with wire, using the pliers to tighten. Repeat with the other three sticks so that you have two triangles.

Lay the two triangles over the top of each other in opposite directions and secure together using the wire and pliers in at least three places where they overlap.

Decorate the star by attaching small pine cones, holly, pine needles or small bells with colourful wool or wire.

Use the stars as Christmas tree decorations, tie them to presents, hang one on your front door or in a window, or make many stars and create a decorative hanger.

advent
CALENDAR

advent
CALENDAR

Advent calendars are a fun way to celebrate the days leading up to Christmas Day. One envelope or parcel is opened each day between 1 and 24 December. Each day there is instructions for an activity or a small gift.

Choose 24 things from our list of ideas on page 115, or create your own. Write these down onto small pieces of paper, place them into envelopes and seal with masking tape. The small gifts can be wrapped in paper or placed in a reusable bag. Label each with a number from 1-24.

To hang on a stick, punch a hole in the top of each envelope and thread onto string, securing with a knot each time to spread the envelopes evenly along the string. Make sure the numbers start at 1 from the bottom and work their way to 24 as the envelope closest to the stick.

santas
+ ELVES

santas
+ ELVES

Use the secateurs to cut the fresh wood into pieces about 5-10cm long. Remove a thin layer of bark in the places you wish to draw using the whittling knife or vegetable peeler. You might like to whittle one end to a point to form a hat shape. Remember to use a glove on the hand holding the wood and always push the knife or peeler away from you when whittling.

Rub the sand paper all over the whittled areas to make the wood very smooth. Then use the paint pens to draw the face and clothes onto the wood.

To add a hat, use the glue gun to stick an acorn cap onto the top and decorate with a bell if you wish.

Christmas
CARDS

Christmas
CARDS

To make a **Christmas tree**, select a green leaf as the body of the tree and trim the sides with scissors to form a triangle Christmas tree shape.

Use the scissors and hole punch to create decorations for your tree using colourful leaves.

Stick the decorations onto the green leaf with glue. Use the paint pens to add more details if you wish.

To make a **reindeer**, use the paint pens to draw a reindeer face onto an orange or brown leaf.

Turn the leaf over and use masking tape to secure two sticks for the antlers and two small leaves for the ears.

To make the Christmas card, fold a piece of seed paper or cardboard in half and use the glue to secure the leaf art onto the front.

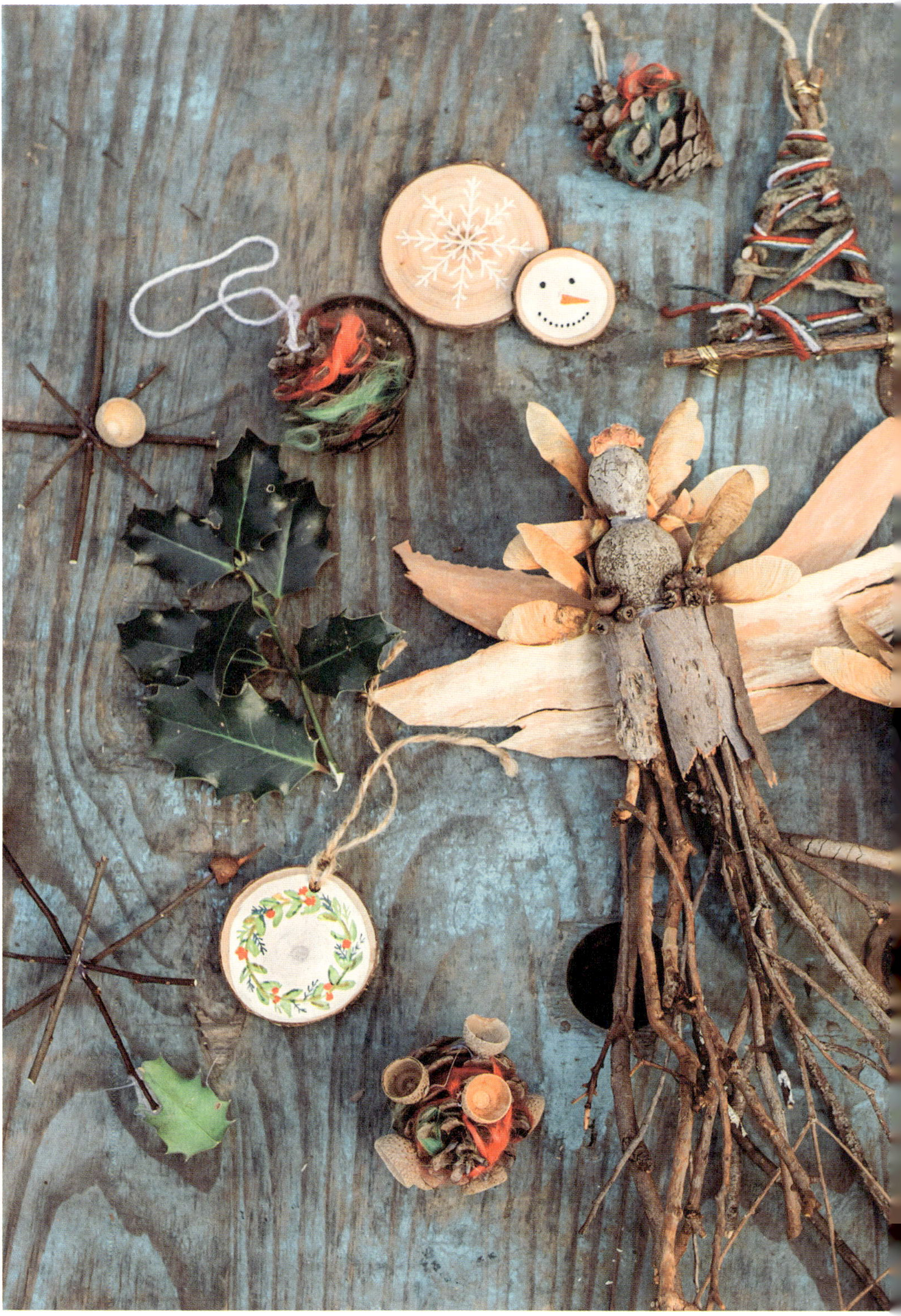

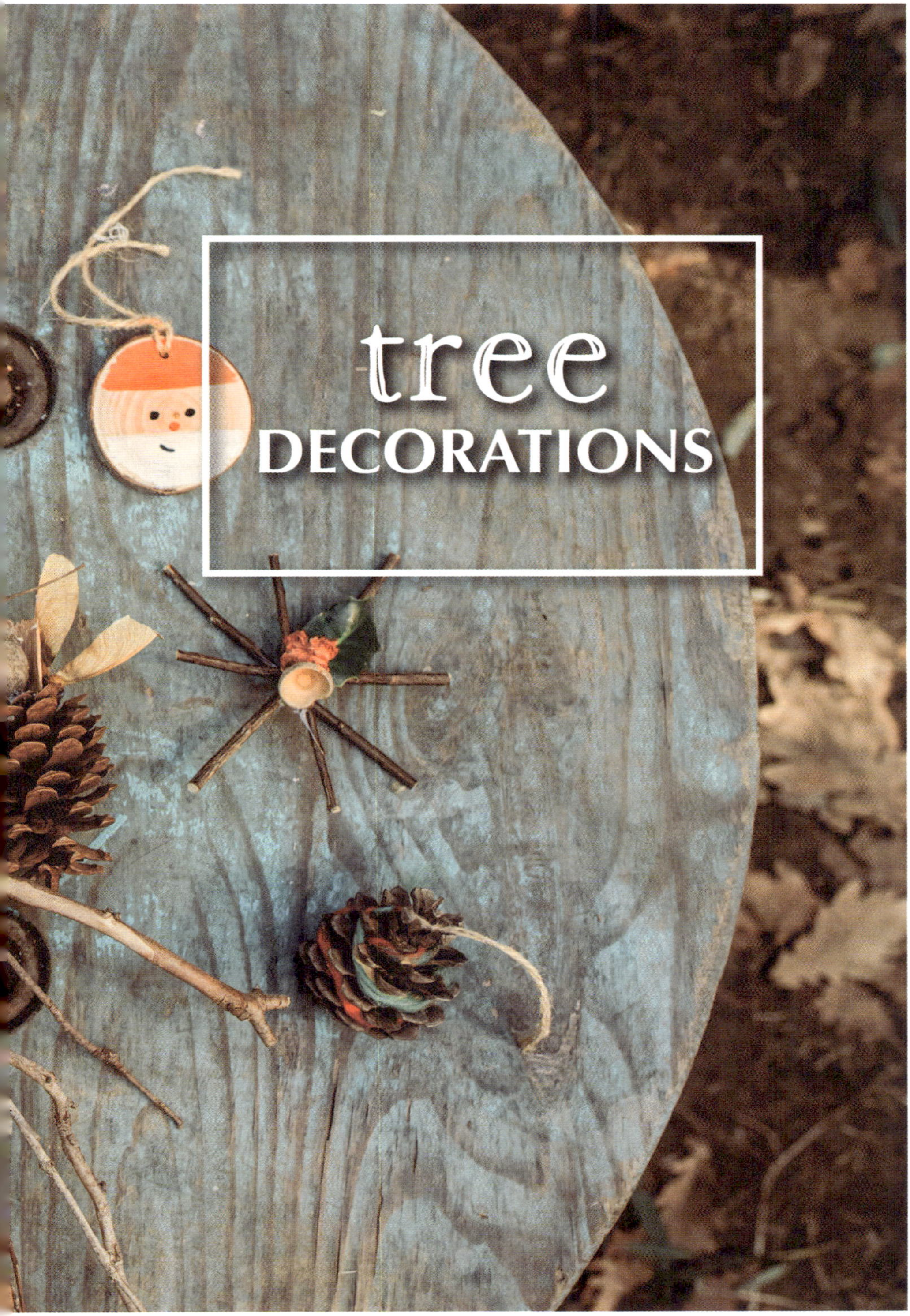
tree
DECORATIONS

tree
DECORATIONS

To make a **Christmas tree** decoration, find two sticks the same length and one stick half the length. Lay them in a triangle and join the corners together with string or wire. Decorate with colourful wool or felt.

To decorate a **pine cone**, rub small amounts of felt into a sausage in your hands and poke into the pine scales.

To make a **snowflake**, find four sticks the same size and glue them together in a star shape using a generous amount of glue from the glue gun. Attach decorations to the snowflake using the glue gun and allow to dry.

Use the paint pens to draw onto the **wood slices**.

Attach a piece of looped string or wool to each of your decorations so they can hang on the Christmas tree.

wild EASTER

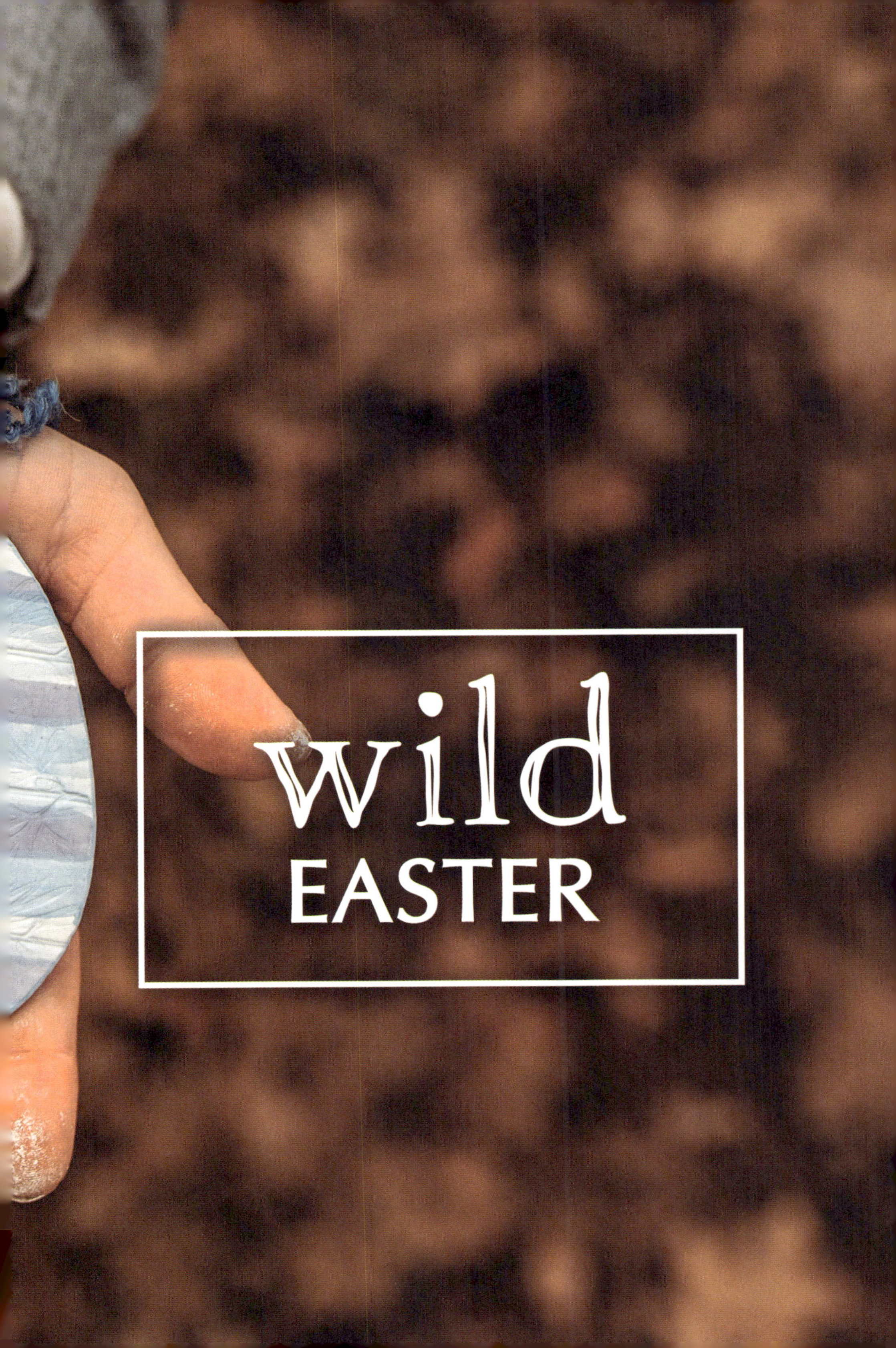

Easter
EGG DYEING

Easter
EGG DYEING

Lay a piece of cheesecloth on the table and place an egg in the centre. Choose some delicate leaves or flowers and trim the stems with scissors. It is best if they are thin as they will stick to the eggs better.

Wet your finger with some of the dye and use it like glue to stick the nature onto your egg. Tightly wrap the cheesecloth around your egg and secure with a twist tie or rubber band.

Submerge the eggs into the natural dye and leave them to soak for two hours or overnight for a deeper colour.

Wearing gloves if you wish, take the eggs out of the dye and carefully remove the cheesecloth and nature. Rinse the eggs briefly under cold water and leave to dry. Try not to touch the egg shells until they are completely dry.

bunny CROWN

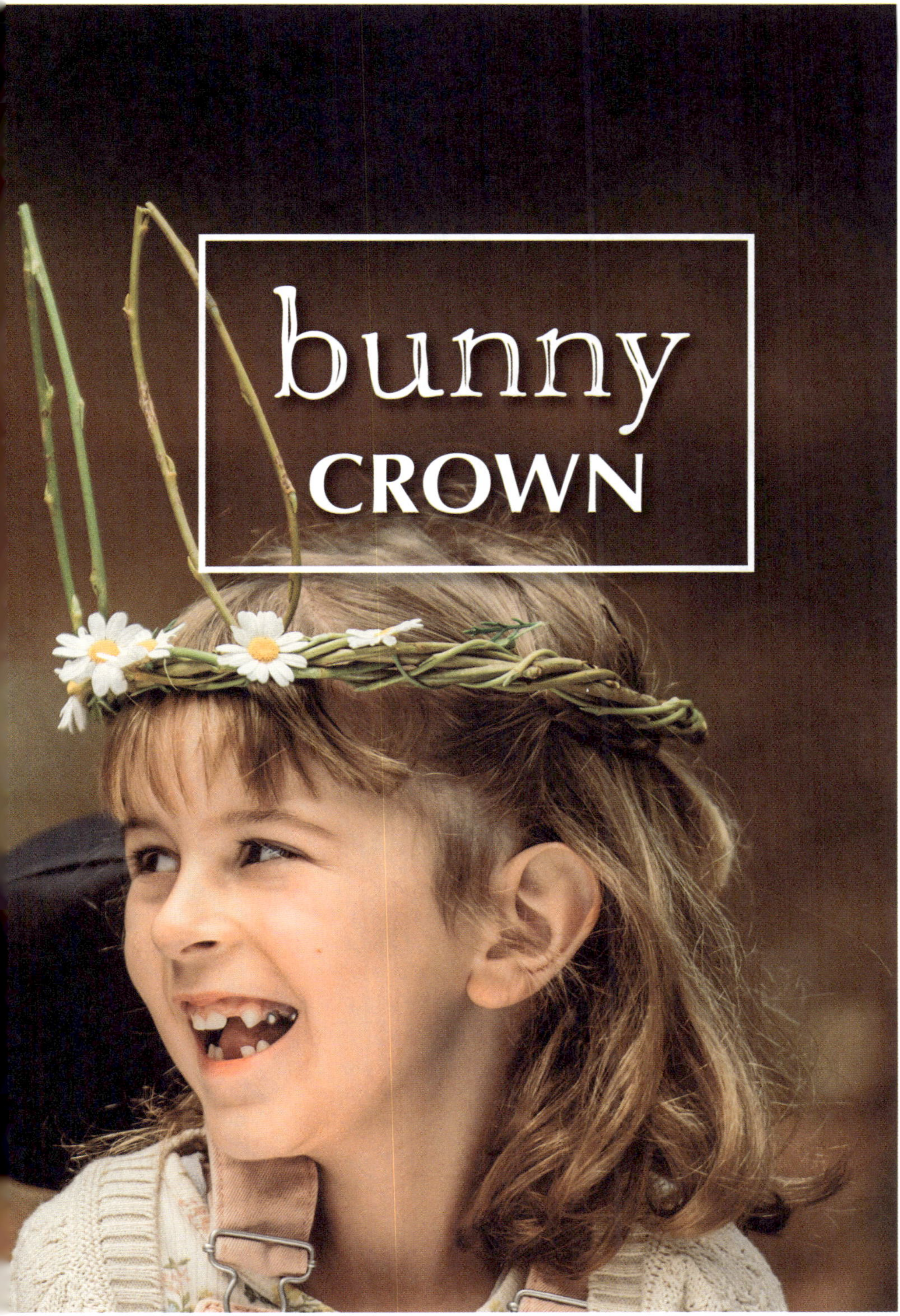

bunny
CROWN

THINGS TO GATHER

Willow branches or bendy nature

Flowers

Secateurs

String, or wire and pliers

*See a video of how to weave your crown base at yourwildbooks.com

Strip the leaves from the willow branches. Measure how big your crown needs to be by wrapping a one-metre piece of willow around your head and cross it over leaving similar lengths hanging down at each end. Hold the cross-over point with your fingers and take it off your head.

Carefully keeping the crown the correct size, weave the hanging ends of the branch in and out of the circle. Add more branches until you have your desired base.

To add ears, gently fold a willow branch in half and poke through the woven willow, then weave the ends of the branch into the crown. Add flowers using the same method to decorate your crown. You can tie the flowers on with wire or string if you wish to make them more secure.

Easter
TREE

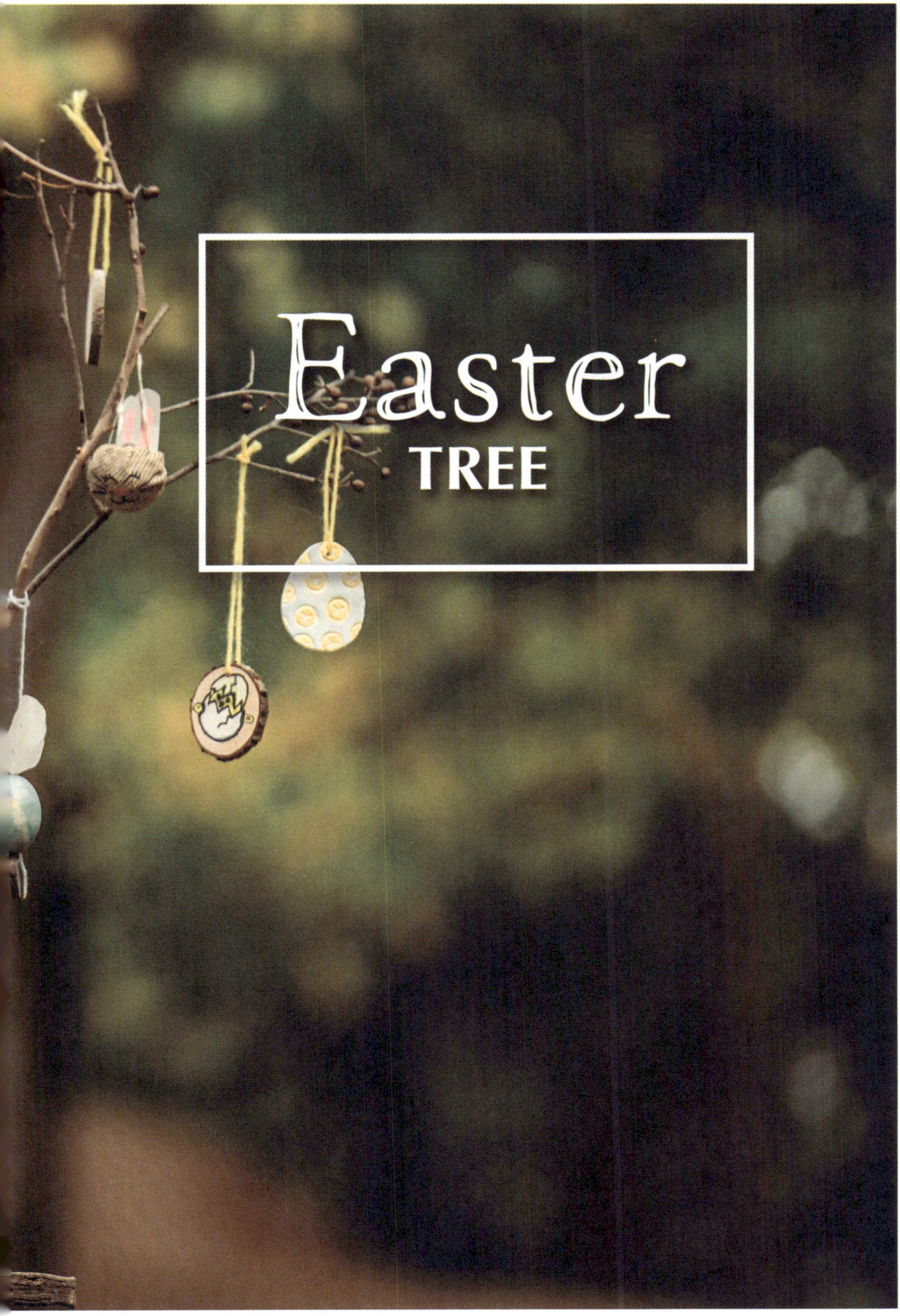

Easter
TREE

To make the tree base, secure the large sticks into the jar of pebbles. Use colourful string to attach Easter themed decorations of your choice. Here are some ideas but feel free to create your own as well.

- Blown eggs that have been coloured in natural dye.
- Air dry clay cut into bunny and egg shapes, decorated with paints, petals and eco glitter.
- Wood slices with Easter drawings on them using paint pens.
- Pine cones decorated with colourful felt to look like Easter eggs.
- Pine cone bunnies.
- Mini nest with egg inside.

pine cone BUNNY

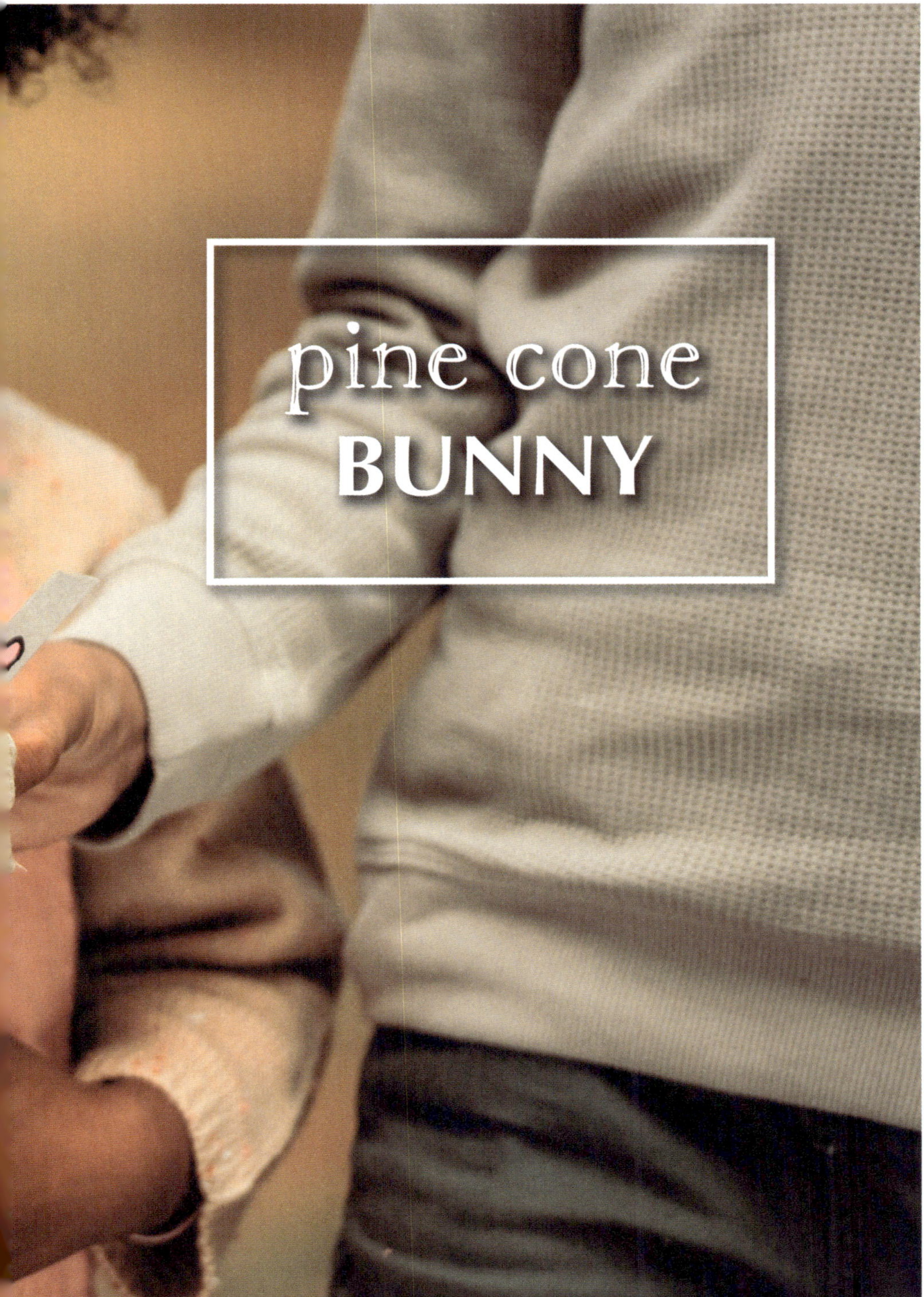

pine cone
BUNNY

THINGS TO GATHER

*Fabric cut to approx
10cm x 10cm*

Paint pens

Pine cones

Rubber bands

Cardboard

Scissors

Cotton balls

Use the paint pens to draw a face on the centre of the piece of fabric.

Wrap the fabric around the large end of the pine cone and secure with a rubber band. Poke the ends of the fabric between the pine cone scales.

Cut the cardboard into two ear shapes with the scissors. Colour the ear with paint pens if you wish. Then poke the ears between the pine scales until secure.

Poke the cotton ball into the pointy end of the pine cone for the tail.

91

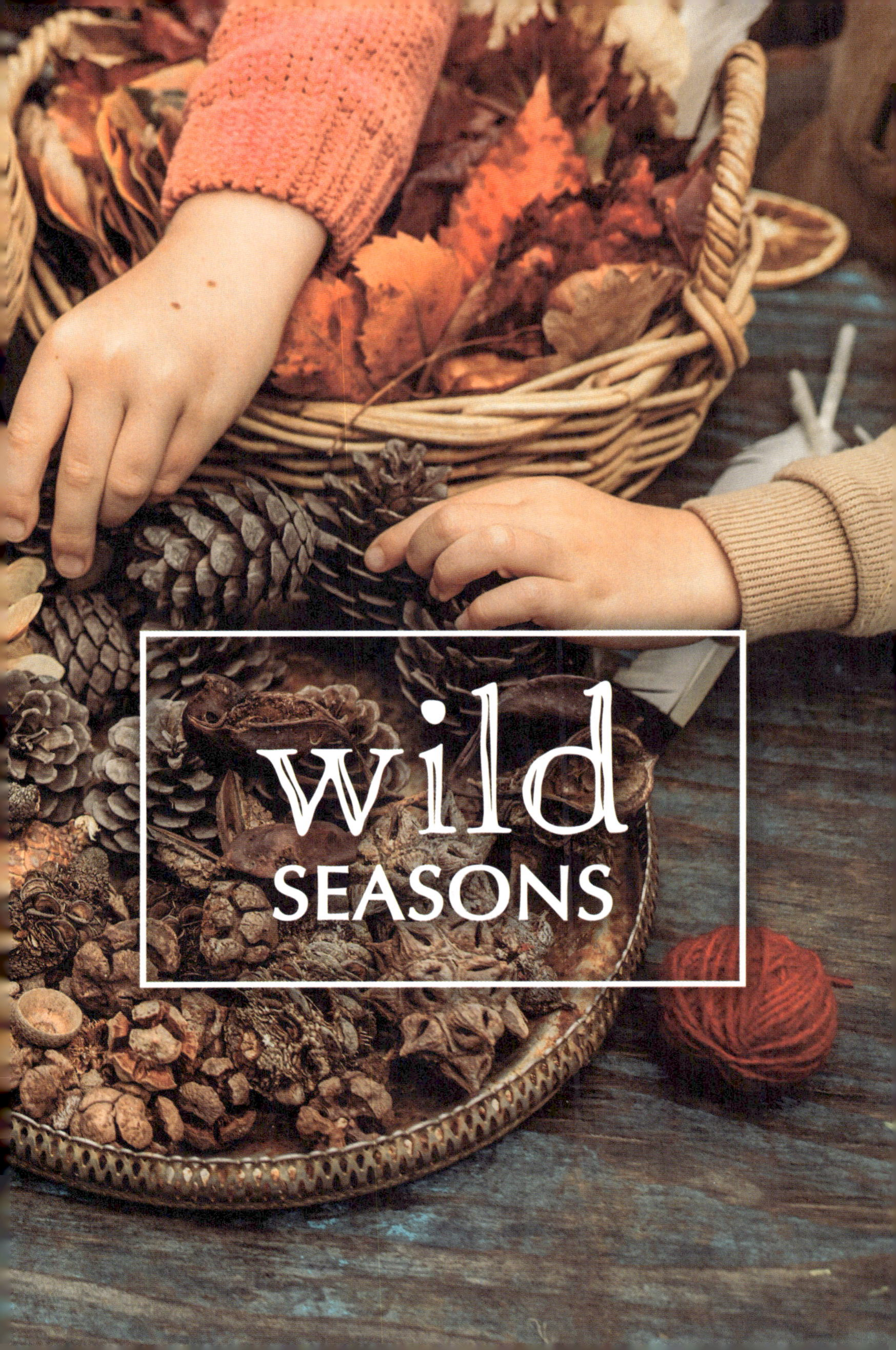
wild
SEASONS

winter
BIRD FEEDER

winter
BIRD FEEDER

THINGS TO GATHER

Glasses or cake tin

Bird seed

Fruit sliced into pieces

Water

String

Scissors

Choose a freezer safe container, such as glasses or a cake tin.

Sprinkle some bird seed into the bottom of your container, then add fruit and more bird seed on top. Gently pour in the water to cover most of the food. Some items can be above the water. Be sure to allow room for the water to expand as it freezes.

Cut a piece of string and make a loop in the end. Place the string into the centre of container so that it forms a hook you can use to hang up the bird feeder when frozen. Place the container into the freezer and leave overnight.

Gently remove the frozen bird feeder from the container. Hang outside in a protected place for the birds to access.

spring
SEED BOMBS

spring
SEED BOMBS

THINGS TO GATHER
Clay
Seed raising soil
Seeds

Use your hands to soften a piece of clay about the size of a walnut, then roll it into a ball.

Flatten the ball of clay onto a hard surface so it is about 0.5cm thick.

Add a small scoop of soil to the middle of the clay, and place a small pinch of seeds onto the soil.

Use you hands to pinch and gather the clay back into a ball so that the soil and seeds remain inside.

Store the seed bombs in a cool, dry place until you are ready to use them.

On a rainy spring day, throw your seed bombs into the garden and with any luck the clay will fall away in the rain and the seeds should sprout and grow!

summer SUNS

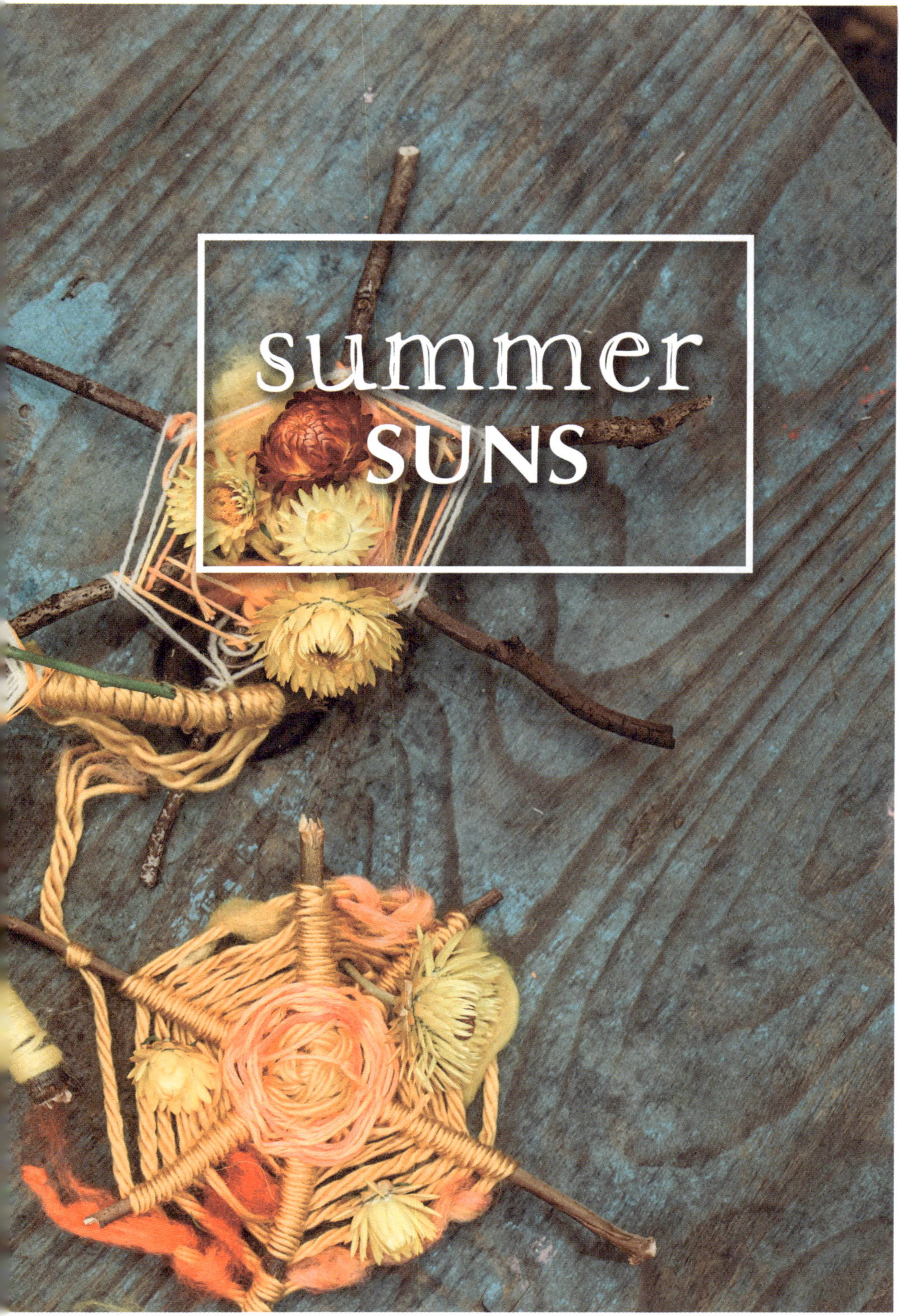

summer
SUNS

Sticks

Scissors

Yellow and orange wool

Yellow and orange felt

Yellow flowers

Find three sticks the same size and lay them on a table with the centre points crossing over. Use the wool to bind them together in the centre so that it looks like a sun shape.

Decorate the sun by winding more wool around the sticks and weaving felt pieces and flowers into the wool.

Hang the sun on your front door like a wreath, or use it to decorate you garden or home.

autumn
HANGER

autumn
HANGER

THINGS TO GATHER

String

Scissors

Sticks

Colourful leaves

Dried orange slices

Various nature such as smal pine cones, acorns, maple seeds and other small seed pods

Cut a length of string about 40-50cm long. Decorate by attaching leaves, dried orange slices and small pieces of nature onto the string. Having a heavier piece of nature on the bottom of the string works well to weigh it down.

Repeat and make another two or three decorated strings.

Tie the decorated strings onto a stick, spacing them evenly to distribute the weight.

Use another piece of string to create a handle so that you can attach your Autumn hanger onto your front door, in a window or in your garden.

wild
EXTRAS

MAKING NATURAL DYE

See **fabric dyeing** (page 26) and **Easter egg dyeing** (page 76) for uses.

THINGS TO GATHER

Fruits and vegetables

Chopping board

Knife

Saucepan and stove

Water

Wooden spoon

Strainer

Glass storage containers

Vinegar

Cut the fruit or vegetable into small pieces about 2-4cm. Bring a saucepan of water to the boil and carefully place food items into the water. Boil gently for approximately 30 minutes, stirring occasionally with a wooden spoon. Allow to cool then use the strainer to remove the food from the liquid. Discard the food into the compost, and pour the natural dye into a glass container for storage (it can stain plastic).

To assist with fastening the colour, add 1/4 cup of vinegar for every litre of dye.

Repeat for each colour using these foods as a guide:

Red cabbage - blue/purple
Beetroot - pink/red
Blackberry - pink/red

Turmeric - yellow/orange
Green - mix turmeric + beetroot dyes

NATURE HUNT GAME BOARD

See page 32 for instructions.

FLYING INSECT

FEATHER

SNAIL OR SLUG

BIRD

CONE OR SEED POD

GRASS

COLOURFUL LEAF

FLOWER

CRAWLING INSECT

Y SHAPED STICK

SPIDER WEB

BUTTERFLY

PARTY PLANNING CHECKLIST

See page 10 for the party preparation guide.

2 MONTHS BEFORE
- Make seed paper for invitations and thank you notes.
- Make decorations such as a party garland (page 18).
- Decide on the party games and craft activities and begin to gather the required items over the next few weeks (see suggestions below).

1 MONTH BEFORE
- Write invitations on seed paper and send to friends.
- Order a cake or plan to make one yourself.
- Check you have suitable vases, a table cloth, crockery, cutlery, a drinks vessel, glassware and serving platters. Borrow from friends or buy second hand.
- Make or buy party favours (page 22).

2-5 DAYS BEFORE
- Buy party food and cake ingredients if needed.
- Forage flowers and foliage from your local area and arrange in vases.

- Compile all items for the party games and craft activities.
- Check RSVPs and make leaf name tags for glasses.

1 DAY BEFORE
- Prepare any food you can (cut fruit, make popcorn) and store appropriately.
- Bake or collect the birthday cake.
- Load the party items into the car or in baskets ready to go to the party location, don't forget a knife to cut the cake, plus candles and matches!

PARTY DAY
- Arrive one hour before the party starts to decorate the area with the fabric garland, and set up the table with vases of flowers, food and drinks.
- Set up the craft activity and organise the games.
- Take photos and have fun!

1 WEEK AFTER
- Send thank you notes using seed paper

PARTY GAMES + CRAFT IDEAS

This is a list of suggested nature craft ideas that you can to do at a birthday party. These ideas are from our other nature play books, but you can also use the activities from this book. Also check the free downloads available on our website at yourwildbooks.com

Activities from *Your Wild Imagination*	Activities from *Your Wild Child*	**GAME IDEAS**
Flower crowns	Nature letters	Nature hunt (page 32)
Pocket press	Earth jewellery	Your Wild Quiz (page 36)
Magic wands	Leaf crowns	Stuck in the mud
Nature masks	Nature weaving	Musical statues
Stick people	Wind catcher	Charades
Story stones	Leaf art	Hopscotch
Tic tac toe	Boats and rafts	Sack race
Magic potions	Light catcher	Capture the flag
		Apple bobbing

YOUR WILD QUIZ GUIDE

Create 38 cards by cutting cardboard into pieces approximately 6cm x 9cm.

Write the 26 letters of the alphabet onto 26 cards and set aside.

Then write the following descriptions onto the remaining 12 cards.

See page 36 for further instructions.

An animal with wings
An animal without wings
A nocturnal animal
An animal that lives in trees
An animal that lays eggs
An animal with no legs

An animal with 2 legs
An animal with 4 legs
A plant
A tree
A flower
A bird

For the purpose of this game, the definition of the word 'animal' includes birds, mammals, insects, reptiles and amphibians, either living or extinct.

A complete version of this game is available to purchase at yourwildbooks.com

ADVENT CALENDAR IDEAS

See page 58 for instructions.

1. Write a letter to Santa
2. Put up your Christmas tree
3. Make a Christmas wreath (p50)
4. Make Christmas tree decorations (p70)
5. Make Christmas mud pies
6. Make a Christmas potion
7. Listen to Christmas carols
8. Make gingerbread cookies
9. Watch a Christmas movie
10. Have a picnic with friends
11. Make gifts for your teachers
12. Attend a local Christmas parade/market
13. Buy food to donate to families in need
14. Donate a toy or book to a local charity
15. Read two Christmas books before bed
16. Make Christmas cards with nature (p66)
17. Send cards to special relatives by mail
18. Make fabric wrapping for presents (p26)
19. Make a Christmas Star (p54)
20. Borrow Christmas books from the library
21. Whittle a Santa from a stick (p62)
22. Draw Christmas story stones
23. Make a wreath for a friend or teacher
24. Make nature tic tac toe as a gift for your friends
25. Make a bird seed feeder as a gift for the birds in your garden
26. Do at least one random act of kindness
27. Take a family photo in front of the tree
28. Film yourselves singing a carol and send it to someone special
29. Have a Christmas music dance party
30. Go for a nature walk wearing a Santa hat

SMALL GIFT IDEAS

Nature craft kits - pine cones, sticks, acorns, seed pods, etc
Crystals or gemstones
Packet of seeds
Eco-friendly bubble wand
Biodegradable glitter
Art supplies
Small ball of wool or felt

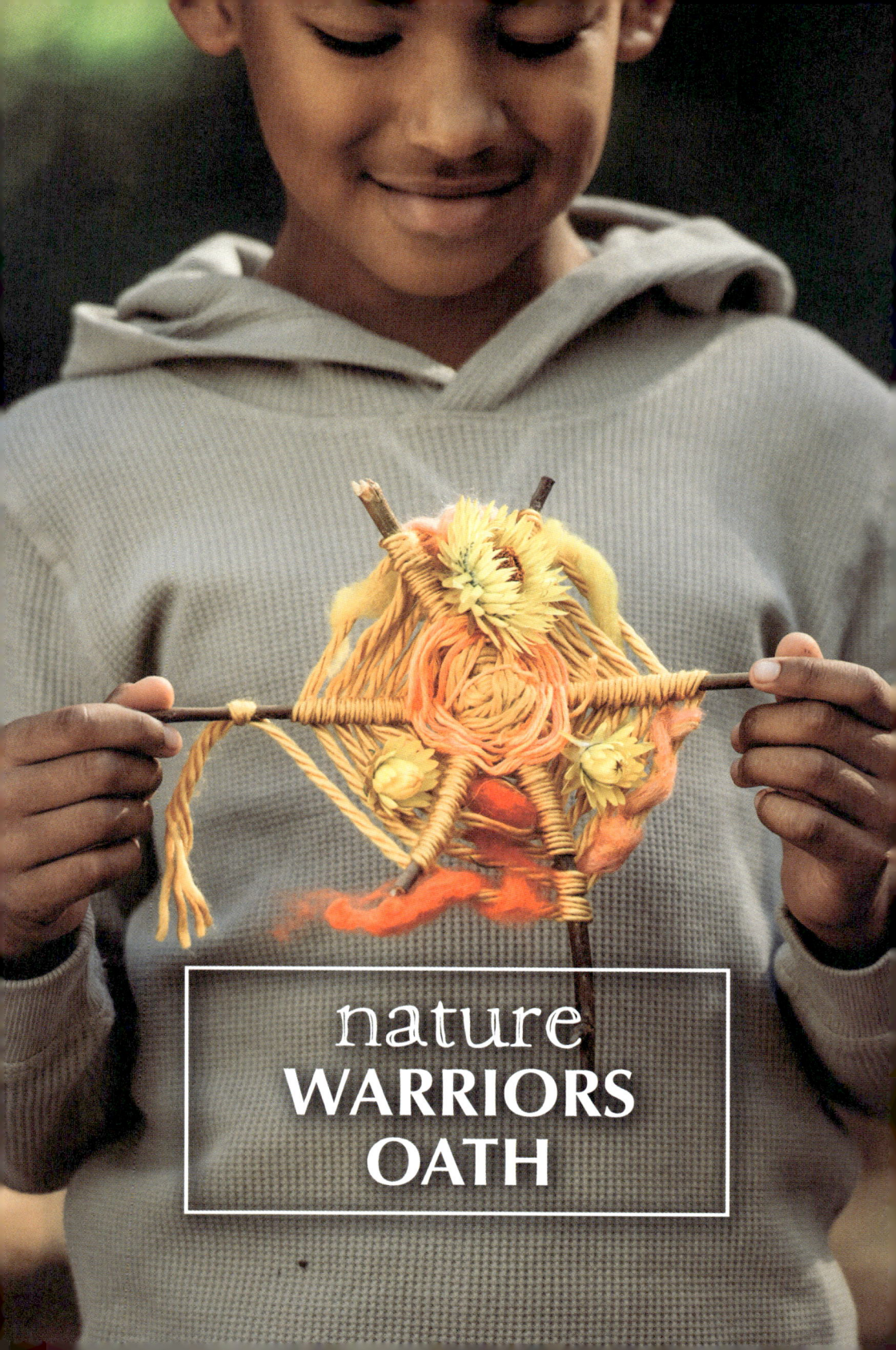

nature
WARRIORS
OATH

Nature Warriors Oath

I am a Nature Warrior
I protect all living things

Plants and animals, soil and air
Beaches and fresh springs

Each day I can make a difference
My choices impact the earth

I refuse, reduce, reuse, recycle
I value nature's worth

I love to have adventures
And play outside with my friends

We appreciate nature's beauty
We climb trees and build dens

We are the Nature Warriors
Together we are strong

We are making change in this world
Our commitment is lifelong.

There are many Nature Warriors in this world. Some are famous, like David Attenborough and Greta Thunberg, but most are regular people like you and me. The world needs millions of people like us who promise to take care of our environment. Are you a Nature Warrior? Say the Nature Warrior's Oath out loud and sign your name here.

....

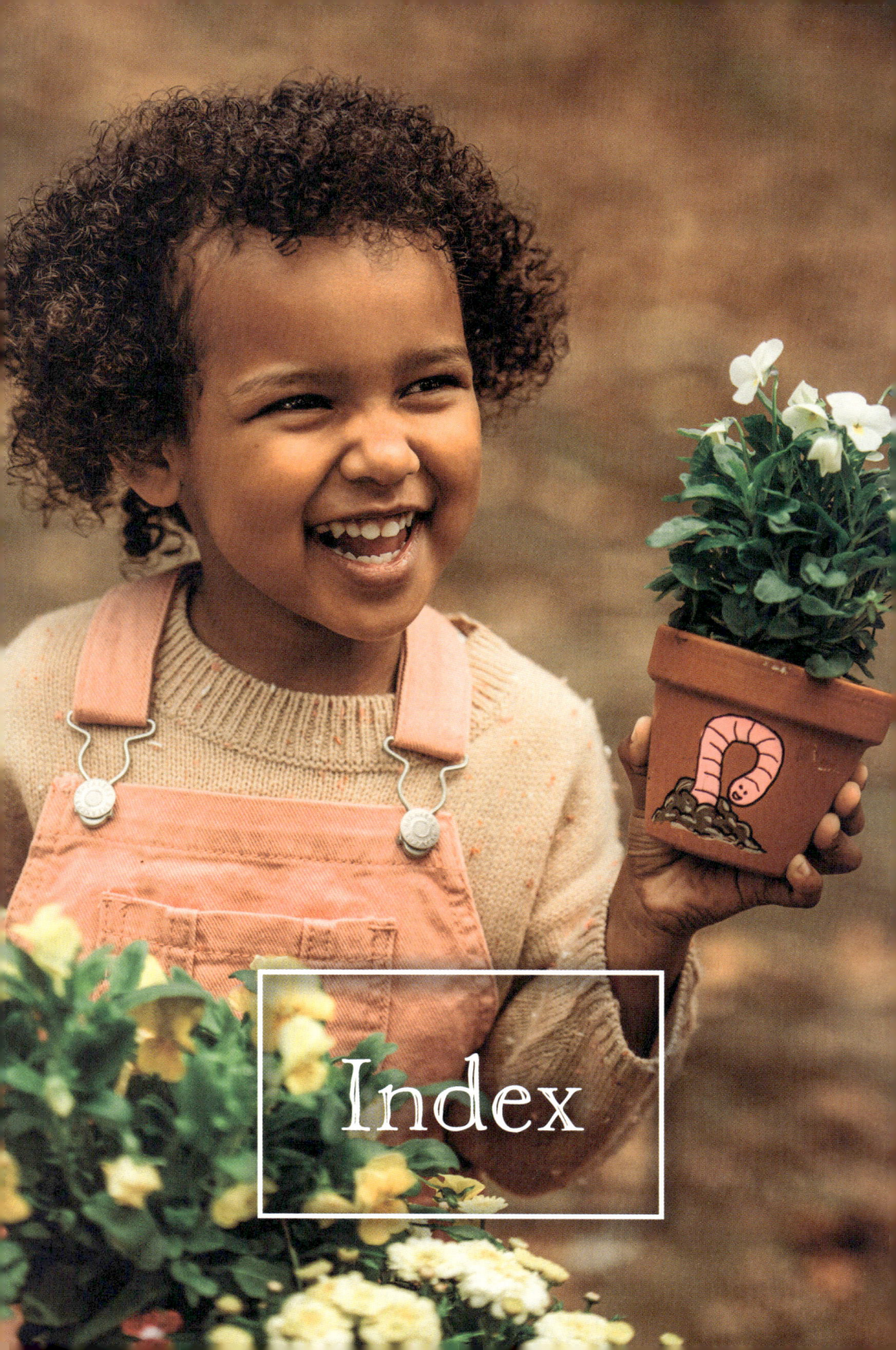

Index

more
RESOURCES

We love sharing ways you can bring more nature into your life on our website, which has a growing range of free resources.

You'll also find some useful videos that can help with the activities in this book, like instructions for how to weave a wreath and crown.

Visit us at **yourwildbooks.com** and join **The Wild Club** newsletter to get all our free resources sent directly to your inbox. Plus, you'll be the first to know about how to get future books.

Our website also includes a small shop, where you can purchase the other books in this series as well as a selection of hand picked items to help you on your nature play journey. We believe in quality over quantity and hope you do too.

YOUR • wild BOOKS

Your Wild Celebration: nature craft for Christmas, Easter, birthdays and more
ISBN 978-0-6486618-4-9

Design, images and text © 2021 by Brooke Davis.
Photography by Megan Crabb.

First published in August 2021.

Also by Brooke Davis
Your Wild Imagination: nature play activities for kids (2019)
Your Wild Child: more nature play activities for kids (2020)
Your Wild Journal: a guided nature journal (2021)
Your Wild Activity Book: nature inspired games and puzzles (2021)

Published by Your Wild Books
PO Box 7452, Hutt Street, SA 5000 Australia

Caring for the environment is central to our values at Your Wild Books, which is why we have chosen to print in Australia using vegetable based inks and FSC certified paper that is manufactured in Australia from responsibly managed forests. This helps to reduce transport emissions, protect forests and reduces chemical use.

Every effort has been made to ensure that the information in this book is accurate at the time of going to print. The author or publisher cannot accept responsibility for any errors or omissions. Please check local regulations prior to undertaking any activities, especially in public spaces. The author or publisher cannot accept any liability for injury, loss, harm or damage to any person or property as a result of following the suggestions in this book.

yourwildbooks.com